Twisters, Tornadoes,
and Other Wild Weather

Pamela Graham

Canadian Edition © 2001 by Scholastic Canada Ltd.
by arrangement with Barrie Publishing Pty Limited

Twisters, Tornadoes, and Other Wild Weather

0-7791-1875-8

Text copyright © Pamela Graham
Momentum Program © Barrie Publishing Pty Limited, 1999

Adapted for Canada by Kevin Polesello

Every effort has been made to contact the owners of the
photographs in this book. Where this has not been possible, we
invite the owners of the copyright to notify the publisher.

AP/AAP: pages 7, 9, 14, 15, 19, 20, 25, 27; ANT Photo
Library/Colin Blobel: 10, 24; ANT Photo Library/J. Burt: 29: ANT
Photo Library/Jack Cameron: 13; ANT Photo Library/A. Krumins:
30: ANT Photo Library/D.V. Matthews: 23; ANT Photo Library/Ted
Mead: 4; I.R. McCann Photo Macdown Productions: 17 (cameo);
ANT Photo Library/Frank Park: 12; ANT Photo Library/Otto Rogge:
5; ANT Photo Library/Silvestris: 26; ANT Photo Library/Wild
Nature: 16; International Photographic Library: cover, title page, 6,
8, 11, 18, 21, 22, 28.

Printed in Canada

10 9 8 7 6 5 4 3   03 04 05

Contents

Introduction

Everywhere we look, we can see signs of how weather has shaped our world. From the smooth rocks in riverbeds, to gently rolling hills, weather has slowly worn down parts of our world. But this process is not always so slow. Sometimes, weather is wild. Wind tears through trees and forces waves to crash with devastating force along the coast. Floods wash bridges and roads away like matchstick models.

All kinds of weather are caused by changes in the temperature of the air. Warm air is lighter than cold air, so it tends to rise. As it rises, cooler air moves in below to take its place. This is how wind is created.

Sometimes, wind swirls around like water running down a drain. In warm climates, fierce winds turn into cyclones and tornadoes. In dry climates, strong winds create dust storms and sandstorms. In cold climates, they bring blizzards.

Rain is created by droplets of water that form into clouds. When water in rivers and oceans becomes warm, some of it evaporates. The warm air, with the water vapour in it, rises. As it goes higher, the air gets cooler, and the vapour begins to turn back into water. These tiny droplets form into clouds. As they move around, they join together and get bigger. When they are heavy enough, they fall to the ground as rain.

Big swirling clouds of moisture can be seen clearly in photos taken by satellites. It is in these clouds that wild weather begins.

This photo taken from space shows swirling masses of clouds in a hurricane.

Cyclones

A tropical storm viewed from space.

Cyclones are massive, rotating tropical storms that are also known as hurricanes and typhoons. They are most common in the warm belt of ocean to the north and south of the equator. They usually begin around areas of low pressure where the surface of the sea is extra warm.

Warm, moist air rushes towards the area of low pressure and swirls around it. As the warm water vapour rises, more warm air rushes in. The tonnes of water vapour form a storm that spins in ever tighter circles as it travels across the ocean, gathering strength with each new rush of warm air. These storm systems can be huge, sometimes 800 kilometres from one side to another.

The centre of this swirling mass is called the eye of the storm. Everything is calm inside the eye, but the rain and wind surrounding it is the worst of the storm. The wind speed can reach 240 kilometres per hour.

Cyclones do their worst damage when they meet the land. The raging winds rip roofs from houses, flatten buildings, and dump torrential rain on coastal land.

A cyclone overturned these mobile homes.

Huge waves created by a storm.

A cyclone often creates huge waves. The low pressure of the eye sucks up a huge mound of water, sometimes eight metres high. On top of this mound, giant waves are whipped up by the winds. The waves rush along until they hit land, washing beaches away, dragging houses into the ocean, and swamping boats. Sometimes, large boats are washed inland. They are found high and dry after the cyclone has swept through.

Cyclones usually die down once they move over land or across a cool area of sea. Heat and moisture are the cyclone's fuel. Once the supply runs out, the cyclone dies down.

Many people in Bangladesh live on the deltas of the Ganges and Brahmaputra Rivers. Each year, cyclones begin in the Indian Ocean and rage across islands in the Bay of Bengal and over the low-lying deltas. They drag massive waves with them and wash away crops, animals, homes, and fishing boats.

Weather forecasts give people time to move to safer ground. In Bangladesh, the government has built solid shelters on thick concrete stilts so people can stay there when wind and rain swamp the area.

Thunder and Lightning

During many storms, thunder and lightning come with the wild wind and rain. Thunderclouds are huge masses of swirling air, water, and ice. These cumulonimbus clouds are grey at the bottom and lighter at the top.

Electricity builds up inside the cloud and escapes as flashes of lightning. The air around a lightning flash instantly becomes five times hotter than the sun. This air expands at supersonic speed and creates the mighty sound of thunder. Light travels much faster than sound does, so we see the lightning before we hear the thunder.

A lightning bolt escaping from cumulonimbus clouds.

A lightning storm brightening up the night sky .

Thunderstorms are common in some hot countries. During summer, dark clouds build up during the day and release thunder, lightning, and heavy rain in the afternoons and evenings.

The spectacular show of lightning, with its rumble and crash of thunder can last for hours. Hundreds of lines of fork lightning zoom between the bottom of the clouds and the ground. Sheet lightning flashes from cloud to cloud. These strikes of lightning brighten the night sky as if it were daytime.

Despite the deafening noise of a thunderstorm, lightning is a friend of the farmers. It releases nitrogen from the air. Raindrops absorb this nitrogen and carry it to the ground. This enriches the soil and helps plants grow.

Storm clouds and lightning over farmland.

Floods

Heavy rain has caused the banks of this river to burst, flooding the land.

Many floods are caused by storms that begin at sea. Big waves from tropical cyclones crash onto coastal regions and swamp the land. These floods happen very quickly and usually drain away quickly, too.

Floods caused by heavy rain over the land usually last longer. In some countries, melting snow is added to the rain. All this water gushes along creeks and rivers, bursting over the banks and spreading over the land. These floods may last for weeks.

13

In China, the Huang He or Yellow River is called "China's sorrow" because of the damage caused by its regular floods. The river seems yellow because earth that is carried down from the upper reaches of the river is a yellowish colour. The flow of the river slows as it gets to the plains, and this yellow earth settles onto the river bed. This makes the river shallower. When heavy rain falls, the water spills over the banks more easily and the swirling floods rush over huge areas of low-lying land.

Flood fighters in China pile up sandbags.

The people living in flat regions along the river have tried to hold back the floods by building raised banks or levees. The power of the rushing water often breaks through them. When some areas flood often or for long periods, the people build temporary bridges so they can walk or ride over the flooded ground.

Although floods cause a lot of damage, the silt they leave on the plains gives the farmers fertile soil for their crops.

Soldiers in China fight flood waters to repair a collapsed levee.

Hailstorms

In certain conditions, the raindrops in clouds can form
into hailstones. Hail is formed high up in turbulent
thunderclouds. Raindrops in the cloud are whipped
around through updrafts and downdrafts in the cloud.
As they pass through layers of cold air, they freeze and
turn into ice pellets. The longer they are whipped
around, the more layers of ice form around them.

Most hailstones are smaller than marbles, but sometimes they can grow to the size of tennis balls. On the North American prairies, hailstones have been known to reach 15 centimetres in diameter.

Hailstorms can cause a lot of damage. Not only do they dent the roofs of cars and damage buildings, they can completely destroy crops. Since hailstorms usually occur in summer, entire fields of corn, wheat, and other crops can be ruined.

Turbulent storm clouds.

Some of these hailstones are over two centimetres in diameter.

Tornadoes

A tornado or waterspout, over the sea.

Tornadoes, whirlwinds, and waterspouts are sometimes called twisters because they whirl around with such force.

Tornadoes start inside huge thunderclouds. They usually start over land, when a mass of warm air is trapped beneath heavier cold air as it heads north. Clouds form and turbulent storms set an uprush of warm air spinning through the cloud. This whirling funnel reaches down from the cloud and eventually touches the ground.

At first, the twister is white with water vapour. Before long, it turns black as dust and debris are sucked up into the moist air. Damage to property is caused by the strong winds gushing around the funnel. These winds have reached 500 kilometres per hour. They are the strongest winds on Earth.

Debris is whirled through the air by this tornado in Texas.

This small building was blown into the middle of the street by a tornado, while others were left standing.

The worst tornadoes happen in the United States. A few hundred tornadoes may strike each year around the area of the Mississippi River. This is known as Tornado Alley. Houses are unroofed and some are completely blown away. Cars, buses, trucks, mobile homes, and planes are tossed around like toys. A tornado once lifted a train off its tracks. Damage is also caused by flying objects like loose wood and bricks.

A tornado may be only a few metres wide where it touches the ground, or it may be a kilometre wide. The average is a few hundred metres. A tornado makes a deafening roar as it traces a path of destruction. At the edges of the tornado's path, property is eerily untouched. One house may be flattened, while the one next to it is left standing.

When the funnel cannot hold any more dust and debris, the dark cloud becomes lighter in colour. The funnel gets narrower and disappears.

Some people in the United States have built underground shelters. They race into them when they see a tornado coming. There is not much else you can do if you live in the path of such wild weather.

A dark tornado full of dust and debris.

Storms in the Desert

A sandstorm at Lake Turkana, Kenya.

Most wild weather comes down from the clouds, but storms in the desert are formed by hot air whirling up from the ground. The clouds of a dust storm are dark and carry sand or dust rather than rain.

The Sahara Desert is the biggest desert in the world. It stretches right across the top of Africa. Huge, dry storms that sweep over the land are gradually changing the shape of the desert. Clouds of sand whirl over the land, shifting tonnes of sand. This reshapes and moves the dunes. These storms often last for days and push sand over roads and villages. They can be so fierce they can blast paint off buildings.

The fine dust picked up by these storms is lighter than the coarse grains of desert sand. They can be whipped up into a cloud of dust up to 3000 metres high. This dust is often lifted up and carried long distances by high-level winds. Red dust from the Sahara Desert has been known to fall to the ground as far away as Italy and France.

People who live in the desert are planting shrubs along the sides of roads to act as barriers to the shifting sand. Farmers make low fences of twigs held together by wire to protect their small crops from wind and sand. They are also planting more trees so the roots will hold the soil together. This will help prevent the precious topsoil being blown away by a desert storm.

A large dust storm in the desert.

Blizzards

Gale-force winds in a blizzard are holding this person up.

In cold climates, wild weather comes in the form of blizzards. A blizzard begins with a gentle fall of snow. When the snow gets thick and the wind turns fierce, the snowfall becomes a blizzard. Blizzards happen in the coldest parts of the world and are common across the north of Europe, Asia, and North America.

In these areas, a blizzard is considered to be any snow storm in which winds blow faster than 51 kilometres per hour and the temperature is below –7°C. In a severe blizzard, winds reach 72 kilometres per hour and the temperature drops below –12°C. In the Antarctic, however, blizzards are much stronger than this. Winds rush across the ice plateau at 160 kilometres per hour and temperatures can drop as low as –89°C.

Sometimes, a blizzard causes snow to be blown into huge piles called snowdrifts. These can block doorways and windows, and cover cars and trains. Some buildings collapse under the weight of ice and snow. Ice forms on power lines and the weight pulls them over, leaving homes without electricity. Pipes freeze and the water inside them turns to ice. Rivers freeze, roads are covered by snow and airports close.

Motorists trapped in a snowdrift.

Sometimes, blizzards pile up huge masses of snow on mountainsides. A sudden sound or movement can cause the snow to move and slide down. When a large amount of snow does this, it is called an avalanche. As it roars down the mountainside, it dislodges more snow, rocks, and trees.

An avalanche in Switzerland.

At the beginning of 1997, a severe blizzard swept across Sweden and Denmark. It uprooted trees, brought down power lines and stopped traffic. The icy winds kept blowing until they spread across parts of Russia. Avalanches blocked both ends of a tunnel, trapping people inside for some time.

This house in Norway was destroyed by an avalanche.

Ice Storms

Another cold-weather phenomenon is the ice storm. Ice storms occur when the temperature of the ground is below freezing. Falling rain turns to ice as soon as it hits the frozen ground. The entire area becomes coated in ice. The visual effect can be very beautiful, with entire forests transformed into sparkling ice sculptures.

Ice and snow cover this road, making driving dangerous.

Although they seem gentle compared to other forms of wild weather, ice storms can still be deadly. Roads and sidewalks are covered in sheets of ice and are hazardous to drive or walk on. Tree branches snap and crash to the ground. Power lines sag under the weight of the ice and then tear apart, often leaving large areas without electricity for warmth and light. A massive ice storm hit Ontario, Quebec, and New Brunswick in 1998.

Icicles hanging from a fence.

Many places in the world are affected by wild weather. People living in these areas have learned to live with the wild conditions that arrive every now and then. Weather forecasters can predict when most storms are coming and how severe they will be. This gives people time to prepare. They can move into special shelters and wait for the wild weather to pass.

Not every storm brings savage destruction. Some storms bring much-needed rain. Floods and lightning replenish nutrients in the soil.

We cannot stop wild weather, but in most cases we can learn to live with it.

A tropical cyclone warning on television.

Glossary

delta a large triangular deposit of earth that forms at the mouth of a river

evaporates water turns into water vapour

forecasts reports telling people what the weather is likely to be

levees human-made banks usually beside a river

nitrogen a colourless gas that makes up about four-fifths of the atmosphere

satellite a manufactured device that orbits Earth

tropical from the tropics, which is the region lying between the Tropic of Cancer and the Tropic of Capricorn

Index